What CIOs Need To Know In Order To Successfully Manage An IT Department

Decision Making Skills That Every CIO Needs To Have In Order To Be Able To Make The Right Choices

"Practical, proven techniques that will show you how to manage your IT department in order to make it successful"

Dr. Jim Anderson

Published by:
Blue Elephant Consulting
Tampa, Florida

Copyright © 2013 by Dr. Jim Anderson

All rights reserved. No part of this book may be reproduced of transmitted in any form or by any means, electronic or mechanical, including photocopying, recording or by any information storage and retrieval system without written permission of the publisher, except for inclusion of brief quotations in a review.

Printed in the United States of America

Library of Congress Control Number: xxx

ISBN-13: 978-1539893592
ISBN-10: 1539893596

Warning – Disclaimer

The purpose of this book is to educate and entertain. This book does not promise or guarantee that anyone following the ideas, tips, suggestions, techniques or strategies will be successful. The author, publisher and distributor(s) shall have neither liability nor responsibility to anyone with respect to any loss or damage caused, or alleged to be caused, directly or indirectly by the information contained in this book.

Recent Books By The Author

Product Management

- Product Development Lessons For Product Managers: How Product Managers Can Create Successful Products

- Customer Lessons For Product Managers: Techniques For Product Managers To Better Understand What Their Customers Really Want

Public Speaking

- How To Rehearse In Order To Give The Perfect Speech: How to effectively rehearse your next speech to that your message be remembered forever!

- Delivering Excellence: How To Give Presentations That Make A Difference

CIO Skills

- How CIOs Can Make Innovation Happen: Tips And Techniques For CIOs To Use In Order To Make Innovation Happen In Their IT Department

- CIO Communication Skills Secrets: Tips And Techniques For CIOs To Use In Order To Become Better Communicators

IT Manager Skills

- Secrets Of Effective Leadership For IT Managers: Tips And Techniques That IT Managers Can Use In Order To Develop Leadership Skills

- IT Manager Career Secrets: Tips And Techniques That IT Managers Can Use In Order To Have A Successful Career

Negotiating

- Learn How To Argue In Your Next Negotiation: How To Develop The Skill Of Effective Arguing In A Negotiation In Order To Get The Best Possible Outcome

- How To Open Your Next Negotiation: How To Start A Negotiation In Order To Get The Best Possible Outcome

Miscellaneous

- Power Distribution Unit (PDU) Secrets: What Everyone Who Works In A Data Center Needs To Know!

- Making The Jump: How To Land Your Dream Job When You Get Out Of College!

Note: See a complete list of books by Dr. Jim Anderson at the back of this book.

Acknowledgements

Any book like this one is the result of years of real-world work experience. In my over 25 years of working for 7 different firms, I have met countless fantastic people and I've been mentored by some truly exceptional ones. Although I've probably forgotten some of the people who made me the person that I am today, here is my attempt to finally give them the recognition that they so truly deserve:

- Thomas P. Anderson
- Art Puett
- Bobbi Marshall
- Bob Boggs

Dr. Jim Anderson

This book is dedicated to my wife Lori. None of this would have been possible without her love and support.

Thanks for the best 21 years of my life (so far)...!

Table Of Contents

JUST EXACTLY HOW DO CIOS MANAGE? 8

ABOUT THE AUTHOR 10

CHAPTER 1: CIO LESSONS FROM THE WAR IN IRAQ 15

CHAPTER 2: RISK MANAGEMENT IN IT: HOW DO YOU DO IT CORRECTLY? 19

CHAPTER 3: WHO YOU GOING TO CALL WHEN IT'S DOWN? NOBODY! 23

CHAPTER 4: HOW CAN IT GET YOUR CFO TO GIVE YOU $$$? 26

CHAPTER 5: WHAT CAN TOYOTA TEACH IT ABOUT HOW TO BE SUCCESSFUL? 30

CHAPTER 6: WHY TOYOTA'S IT DEPARTMENT IS BROKEN & WHY THAT'S OK 33

CHAPTER 7: HOW TOYOTA CAN TEACH IT TO KEEP THINGS FRESH ... 37

CHAPTER 8: WHAT TOYOTA CAN TEACH IT ABOUT DEALING WITH CHANGE 41

CHAPTER 9: CITI SHOWS HOW NOT TO RUN AN IT DEPARTMENT 44

CHAPTER 10: HOW TO DRIVE AN IT DEPARTMENT INTO THE GROUND 48

CHAPTER 11: 3 SECRETS THAT OIL COMPANIES USE TO RUN A GREAT IT DEPARTMENT 51

CHAPTER 12: CAN'T WE ALL JUST GET ALONG (IN IT)? 54

Just Exactly How Do CIOs Manage?

At the heart of being a CIO is the responsibility to manage an entire department of technical professionals. It is your job to provide an overall direction for the department to move in and when problems arise, and they always do, you are going to have to work with your staff in order to create solutions.

How to accomplish all of this can be a real challenge. However, clever CIOs realize that they can get helpful tips from the military based on the how they've handled the conflict in Iraq. CIOs also understand that running an IT department is filled with risk – many things can and will go wrong. This means that they need to become adept at risk management.

Nothing is going to get accomplished if you don't have the funding to accomplish it. This means that a critical CIO skill is the ability to get funds allocated to you from the CFO. This is what you're going to need in order to keep everything up and running like it should be.

Taking the time to look around can provide you with an opportunity to discover well run IT shops that can provide you with suggestions on how you can run your IT department. A great place to look is Toyota's IT department which does a fantastic job of dealing with change as it happens.

In order to keep an IT department operating correctly, we need to understand what could cause it to be run into the ground and then avoid doing those things. Once again, looking for suggestions from well-run IT departments such as those found at the large oil companies can show us the way.

For more information on what it takes to be a great CIO, check out my blog, The Accidental Successful CIO, at:

www.TheAccidentalSuccessfulCIO.com

Good luck!

- Dr. Jim Anderson

About The Author

I must confess that I never set out to be a CIO. When I went to school, I studied Computer Science and thought that I'd get a nice job programming and that would be that. Well, at least part of that plan worked out!

My first job was working for Boeing on their F/A-18 fighter jet program. I spent my days programming fighter jet software in assembly language and I loved it. The U.S. government decided to save some money and went looking for other countries to sell this plane to. This put me into an unfamiliar role: I started to meet with foreign military officials and I ended up having to manage groups of engineers who were working on international projects.

Time moved on and so did I. I found myself working for Siemens, the big German telecommunications company. They were making phone switches and selling them to the seven U.S. phone companies. The problem was that the switches were too complicated. Customers couldn't tell the difference between one complicated phone switch from another complicated phone switch. Once again I found myself working with the sales and marketing teams to find ways to make the great technology that the engineers had developed understandable to both internal and external customers.

I've spent over 25 years working as an senior IT professional for both big companies and startups. This has given me an opportunity to learn what it takes to manage and IT department in ways that allow it to maximize its output while becoming a valuable part of the overall company.

I now live in Tampa Florida where I spend my time managing my consulting business, Blue Elephant Consulting, teaching college courses at the University of South Florida, and traveling to work with companies like yours to share the knowledge that I have about how to create and manage successful IT departments.

I'm always available to answer questions and I can be reached at:

Dr. Jim Anderson
Blue Elephant Consulting
Email: jim@BlueElephantConsulting.com
Facebook: http://goo.gl/1TVoK
Web: www.BlueElephantConsulting.com

"Unforgettable communication skills that will set your ideas free..."

Create IT Departments That Are Productive And A Valuable Asset To The Rest Of The Company !

Dr. Jim Anderson is available to provide training and coaching on the topics that are the most important to people who have to manage IT departments: how can I build a productive IT department (and keep it together) while at the same time providing the rest of the company with the IT services that they need?

Dr. Anderson believes that in order to both learn and remember what he says, speakers need to laugh. Each one of his speeches is full of fun and humor so that what he says "sticks" with everyone.

Dr. Anderson's CIO SkillsTraining Includes:

4. How to identify and attract the right type of IT workers to your IT department.
5. How to build relationships with the company's senior management in order to get the support that you need?
6. How to stay on top of changing technology and security issues so that you never get surprised?

Dr. Jim Anderson works with over 100 customers per year. To invite Dr. Anderson to work with you, contact him at:

Phone: 813-418-6970 or
Email: jim@BlueElephantConsulting.com

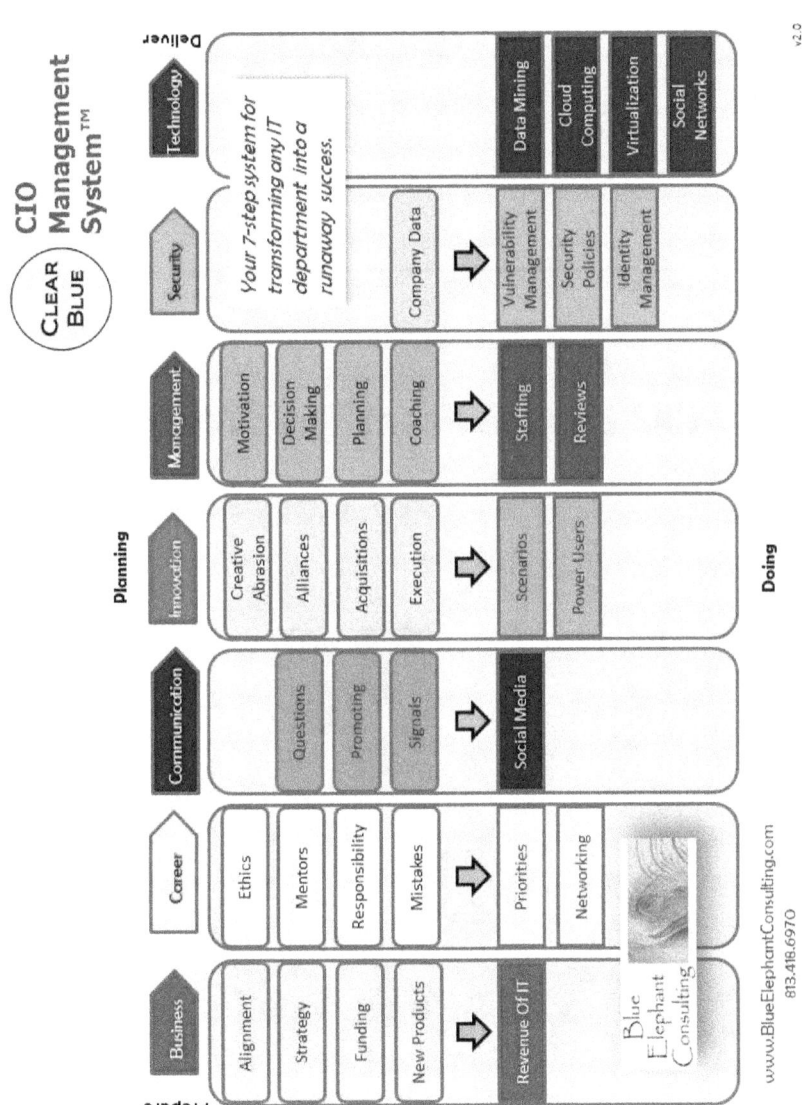

The **Clear Blue CIO Management System™** has been created to provide CIOs and senior IT managers with a clear roadmap for how to manage an IT department. This system shows CIOs what needs to be done and in what order to do it.

Chapter 1

CIO Lessons From The War In Iraq

Chapter 1: CIO Lessons From The War In Iraq

First off, this post has nothing to do with politics. It really does not matter how you feel about the war in Iraq – this post will still contain valuable information for you. I've just gotten done reading the book The Strongest Tribe: War, Politics, and The Endgame In Iraq by Bing West. It's a great book and I highly recommend that you read it. If, just for a moment, we can step away from all of the emotion that talking about this war causes, then we just might be able to realize that this conflict has the opportunity to show CIOs how to run their departments better. Don't believe me? Then read on...

The war in Iraq has pitted a large successful country (the U.S.) against a collection of small, scrappy forces that included Shia, Sunnis, al-Qaeda in Iraq, and probably a bunch of other folks. For a variety of reasons, this conflict has dragged on for over 5 years and only now is the U.S. starting to emerge as the clear victor.

From a CIO perspective, the feeling that one is involved in a conflict with other firms that seem to morph and change shape on a daily basis should feel very familiar. Traditionally IT departments have been able to go toe-to-toe with their competition and either out-spend them on the latest technology or out-hire them in order to get the best talent. In doing this, they could then go to their customers and "prove" that they were the best IT department around.

Now that we are living in the 21st Century, things are not so simple any more. The U.S. forces have the challenge of trying to protect the Iraqi people while fighting the insurgents. IT departments have a similar challenge in that they are trying to serve both their internal and external customers while trying to fight off the threat of being completely outsourced or losing customers to competitors. The U.S. forces can't always tell if the people that they are trying to protect are grateful for the help or so resentful that they are the ones who are taking shots at them. Likewise, a CIO can't be sure if the customers that he's trying to service are working with him or if they are actively trying to replace either him or his entire department!

In Bing West's book, he points out the interesting fact that how to win the war in Iraq was known by the U.S. military based on their experience in Vietnam over 40 years ago. It just took them 5 years to relearn what they already knew. Bing writes that in order to secure Iraq, the U.S. forces needed to follow a seize, secure, rebuild process. This meant that U.S. forces would move into a hostile area, take it over, stay there and provide protection for the locals, and then start to rebuild the area in order to show the locals that the U.S. forces were the good guys. This was a difficult lesson for a force that had been trained to take territory and kill enemies to learn.

Today's CIOs can learn a lot from this hard won information. Specifically, they too need to follow a process of seize, secure, and rebuild in order to make their IT departments successful. Two types of territory can be seized: internal and external. Internal territory is controlled by departments and the more departments that IT interacts with, the more territory it can "seize". Once IT becomes responsible for new tasks / territories, then the real work begins – securing it. This means that the IT department needs to become so good at handling this area and resolving issues quickly that nobody can imagine anyone else handling this task. Additionally, external territory is controlled by customers. If IT can interact with a customer and forge a positive partnership with them, then additional territory will have been seized. Once again, by forming a strong bond between the external customer and the IT department this territory will have been secured.

The final step, rebuilding, is the most important. The U.S. forces found that if they didn't rebuild the territory that they had seized, then the locals would continue to help the bad guys. However, if rebuilding was done, then the locals shunned the bad guys and sided with the Americans.

Having secured new territory, a CIO has to quickly start rebuilding their IT environment. This can be as simple as upgrading their hardware or as complex as creating and delivering a completely new application. The CIO needs to spend time in the new territory finding out what his new customer's needs are. He then needs to solve those needs and make sure that the customer agrees that the problems have been solved. By doing this he will show the customer that the IT department is committed to making their life better.

Seize, secure, and rebuild. How much more simple can this possibly be? Today's CIO has a very clear roadmap to follow in order to be successful.

Chapter 2

Risk Management In IT: How Do You Do It Correctly?

Chapter 2: Risk Management In IT: How Do You Do It Correctly?

The financial melt-down of 2008 had at its core one simple mistake that a whole bunch of companies made at the same time: they did a lousy job of risk management. They made investments in things that were very risky without realizing just how risky they really were. IT departments face the same challenges: at the start of each year we have a number of different projects that we could possibly work on; however, we rarely if ever do a good job of evaluating the risk associated with each of these projects. Instead we focus on things like ROI, business alignment, and which Sr. VP is sponsoring the project to make our decisions. If we don't want to get caught in our own special version of an IT meltdown, then we had better see if we can figure out a way to measure the risk of an IT project...

So what is risk when you are talking about an IT project? In the simplest terms risk is the chance that an IT project will fail to produce the results that you are expecting because of a given event or set of events. The purpose of risk management is to make sure that you fully understand the risks associated with a project before you start it as well as managing those risks while you are working on the project.

In the world of IT projects, risk is more often then not associated with the company data that we are in charge of collecting, maintaining, and processing. IT teams need to retrain themselves to focus on the value of the data that an IT project is going to be processing and then determine the likelihood that the project won't be able to do the processing, or in the worst case will corrupt or lose some / all of that data.

What's really interesting is that outside of IT, the rest of the business has always used risk analysis to determine when they should roll out new products, determine how to spend marketing budgets, and pick which capital investments they want to make. Implementing a good risk management practice within the IT department is yet another way that CIOs can better align their departments with the rest of the business.

Risk management needs to be baked into all of the steps in your IT department's projects. This runs from project planning all the way to post-production. Everyone knows that fixing a risk earlier in the process is much cheaper than trying to fix it later on down the line.

How much is all of this going to cost? Actually, a fair amount if you end up doing it correctly. You're going to have to spend money to determine the value of proposed projects, product lines, and any proposed services. Next you'll have to assign risks to each of these. This can be quite time consuming; however, the process will pay off over time. The key is to have a strategy for how you want to go about doing this. Focusing on where you want the IT department to be in 5 years is a key part of the process because you want whatever project you select to help you to get there.

How can you tell if all of this effort is worth it? There are actually three ways to go about doing this. Most firms use internal audits in order to determine if their IT risk management activities are are paying off. Depending on the industry that you work in, another way is to use regulatory compliance as your measure. Finally, external audits are an expensive but more complete way to measure your effectiveness.

In most IT departments that have an effective risk management function, the funding for the activity comes out of the IT budget. In most companies the belief is that a well-executed risk management program will end up saving them money.

In the end, a risk management program will help your IT department to choose the right projects to work on. Once those projects are selected, then it will help you to develop risk mitigation policies, and fix risk vulnerabilities that may end up yielding process efficiencies. It goes without saying that all of this can end up helping a company meet its regulatory compliance needs.

Chapter 3

Who You Going To Call When IT's Down? NOBODY!

Chapter 3: Who You Going To Call When IT's Down? NOBODY!

Quick question: does your IT department have a business continuity plan? If you don't or, even worse, if you're not sure then basically you are going to eventually lose your job. How many of us work in a building that at least once a year has a fire drill? We all look around, stand up and go outside where we mill around for 15 minutes before they let us back in the building (except for those folks who use this as an opportunity to take off for the rest of the day!) Gosh, if we are willing to do that much work to prepare for a fire, shouldn't we doing at least as much to prepare for something happening to our IT systems?

I suspect that if you talk to any firm that works in New Orleans or New York City, they probably have a IT business continuity plan – they've learned the hard way just how valuable one of these is. Now for the rest of us, what are we waiting for – the eventual arrival of Bird Flu?

Once of the big problems that IT has is that we never remember to budget for a disaster plan. It turns out that these things actually do cost money and they take time and planning to put in place. We end up buying more boxes, wireless access points, and PDAs and then the money is all gone and we still don't have a disaster plan.

So how should an IT department go about creating a disaster recovery plan even if they have very little funding? Simple, assign responsibility to a group of IT staffers and then give them an outline of what they need to create. What they basically need to do is to identify all of the IT processes that your department uses to run the business. Next, they need to prioritize which ones are critical and MUST NOT GO DOWN, or at least need to be the first ones to come back up. The result of this type of internal inspection can be quite surprising. More than one firm has come to realize that the processes that they thought were mission critical were instead nice to haves and the processes that they had not been paying attention to were in reality the ones that they could not afford to do without.

The difference between a disaster recovery plan which everyone gives lip service to and a business continuity plan is that you can take months or even years to implement a disaster recovery plan. However, an IT business continuity plan tells you what you are going to be doing in order to keep the firm's doors open the day after a disaster strikes. In other words, it deals with a much shorter timeframe. In these darkest hours, everyone in the firm is going to be running around trying to figure out what to do. This is the time that a CIO and an IT team that has planned ahead can really shine.

Everyone will remember you if you have a good IT business continuity plan. Oh, and they will REALLY remember you if you don't...!

Chapter 4

How Can IT Get Your CFO To Give You $$$?

Chapter 4: How Can IT Get Your CFO To Give You $$$?

It is a sad fact of the IT world that everything requires money. No matter how cool the new technology would be to have, no matter how critical the update or change may be, you are not going to be getting or doing anything about it unless you have the funds to spend.

In the modern corporation, all funds start in the office of the Chief Financial Officer (CFO). He/she reports to the CEO and at the end of the day, no money flows in the company unless the CFO says that it can. Darn it – can't he/she see how critical your IT project is and just give you the funding that you need?

Elizabeth Millard over at Baseline magazine took the time to talk with CFOs in order to find out what we IT'ers need to do differently. It turns out that what we have here is a failure to communicate. Specifically, we in IT have a bad habit of telling the CFO what we are trying to do and our proposals are generally not very well put together.

What we seem to be failing to do is to look at how a CFO views the world. Everyone is coming to him/her asking for funding. They need to come up with a way to quickly accept or reject a request.

If a proposal crosses their desk that has the support of the CEO, then it has a pretty good chance of getting funded. However, if the proposal that the CFO is looking at is a low priority project or if the proposal is lacking any sort of clear time line for showing results, then you can pretty much forget about it being funded.

The burden of clearly explaining what an IT project is going do in simple, straightforward business language is the responsibility of the IT department – it's not the CFO's responsibility to learn our language. At the end of the day, we need to be able to describe what impact on the firm's business goals, security, customer relationships, and worker productivity is going to be.

In order to capture the CFO's attention, we need to be able to talk to them in terms that will catch their attention. This means that every IT project needs to be able to do three things simultaneously: minimize IT staffing levels, increase customer satisfaction, and (of course) save the firm money.

In the world of corporate finance, surprises are most unwelcome. A proposal should never show up on a CFO's desk without having been well advertised in advance. This means that you need to set up a regular set of meetings between the CFO and IT management in order to keep the CFO appraised of IT challenges and initiatives.

IT and the finance department actually have a lot in common. Both are committed to making the company successful. Areas of overlap include managing services provided by the firm, storage of company records, disaster recovery and business continuity planning, regulatory compliance and discovery initiatives, and security.

No IT project ever gets done in a flash – there are always phases to our projects. These phases need to be carefully spelled out to the CFO and the value to the firm that the project will provide at the end of each phase needs to be clearly stated.

One final thought: a great way to get a CFO to NOT approve your project is to tell the CFO that the project is urgent and then ask him / her to quickly make a decision. More often than not they will – NO!

Take your time and talk with the CFO to make sure that he/she understands how much the project will cost, what risks it comes with, and what you expect the outcome to be. This is your best path to getting the CFO to approve the IT funding that your projects so desperately need.

Chapter 5

What Can Toyota Teach IT About How To Be Successful?

Chapter 5: What Can Toyota Teach IT About How To Be Successful?

You would think that building cars and running an IT department wouldn't have a lot in common and in fact were two completely different activities. However, there are more similarities than are obvious on a first glance. Toyota currently makes some the best products available, they do it at the lowest costs, and they have the ability to develop new products quickly. What IT department wouldn't want to be able to say the same about itself?

At the heart of Toyota's success is its Toyota Production System (TPS). Countless books, papers, and research reports have been written about TPS as everyone from other car companies to pharmaceutical companies have tired to copy Toyota's methods in order to emulate their success.

Hirotaka Takeuchi, Emi Osono, and Norihiko Shimizu have spent the past six years studying what makes Toyota a success and they've come away with some interesting lessons that apply very well to IT departments. One of the things that they discovered is that the TPS is a key part of Toyota's success, but their corporate culture is just as much if not more responsible for Toyota being successful.

In many IT departments, once we get something working correctly, be it a process or an application, we tend to leave it alone and focus on other issues and problems. At Toyota they have developed an environment in which there are constant contradictions and paradoxes that don't allow any solution to remain stagnant for long.

What this means for Toyota employees is that they find themselves having to deal with challenges and problems all of the time. This requires them to learn how to constantly create new and novel ideas that allow them to solve these challenges. The result of all of this innovative thinking is that Toyota is always constantly getting better. What IT department wouldn't kill to be able to say that?

Here's the part that so many companies that study Toyota miss: at Toyota they don't believe that efficiency by itself can guarantee that Toyota will be a success. Instead, Toyota believes that its long-term success lies in its workers. It believes that the wisdom of its workers is what will allow it to improve.

Since its workers are its knowledge repositories, Toyota takes the time to invest in its workers and in its organizational capabilities. This is not a one-way street. Instead, Toyota is also open to new ideas no matter where they come from: production, development, sales, etc.

The folks studying Toyota also discovered a hidden truth: when workers are forced to deal with different ways of looking at a problem because of opposing insights, then this is when they will better understand the problem and are more likely to come up with new and novel solutions to the issue.

Next time we'll talk about Toyota's culture of contradictions and why something that looks like it should screw things up actually helps Toyota to move ahead faster than its competition.

Chapter 6

Why Toyota's IT Department Is Broken & Why That's Ok

Chapter 6: Why Toyota's IT Department Is Broken & Why That's Ok

Over at Toyota, they have a habit of doing things differently than everyone else. This might be one of the reasons that Toyota is such a successful company. Their IT department, just like the rest of the company, looks like it on the brink of failure even as the company does better and better in the marketplace. How can this be?

If you look at the numbers, Toyota has nothing to write home about. They pay very low dividends and it sure looks like they are hording cash – both of these are generally signs of a company that is not being run all that well.

Toyota is just a flat out weird company. Their departments do things that you won't see at any other company. Perhaps there is something that we can learn from how they do things – we would all like to be as successful as they are.

Here are six Toyota oddities that we can puzzle over and perhaps learn from:

1. **Toyota Moves Like A Turtle, But Jumps Like A Rabbit:** It sure seems like Toyota behaves just like you would expect a big firm to behave most of the time: they started making cars in the U.S. through a partnership with GM in 1984 and slowly expanded from there. No big deal. However, then all of a sudden they created and introduced the Prius – a massive jump in technology. Clearly this big firm has start-up type characteristics when needed.

2. **Can I Have Some Change Please?:** If there is once constant at Toyota, it's change. The direction from the top on down is to always be looking for a better way to

do things. Employees are supported in taking risks by management that likes to say "No change is bad!"

3. **What Are You Doing Here?:** So much for lean meetings – at Toyota, most meetings are packed with people no matter whether they have something to say on the topic or not. Toyota also packs its field offices (close to the customers) with staff instead of keeping them at HQ. Finally, senior management seem to be always on the road visiting dealers. Gosh, what a novel concept – stay in touch with all parts of the company!

4. **Penny Wise, Pound Foolish:** Toyota appears to be in another competitive race – they seem to be trying to match Walmart for the honor of being called the cheapest company in the world. At Toyota they flip off the lights over lunch and in Japan they've moved everyone into one big room to work together with no partitions. This counting of pennies is matched by the immense spending that Toyota indulges in on its plants and in training for its employees. All that flipping off of the lights must be working because somehow Toyota has come up with $170M/year to spend on sponsoring a Formula 1 team!

5. **Can You Hear Me Now?:** Instead of trying to impress everyone with your big fancy words, if you worked at Toyota you would be encouraged to communicate using simple, clear expressions. Summaries would be an important part of any slide deck that you put together. However, at the same time you would be encouraged to meet and interact with as many people as possible – other departments, other business units, and other locations. Can you imagine how long your IM list would be?

6. **Do What The Boss Says, Or Not:** It's not what you would expect to find at a Japanese company, but at Toyota employees are encouraged to "Pick a friendly fight". Employees are encouraged to speak up and contradict what their bosses have told them to do. Don't do what your boss told you to do just because he/she told you to do it!

Chapter 7

How Toyota Can Teach IT To Keep Things Fresh

Chapter 7: How Toyota Can Teach IT To Keep Things Fresh

Despite all the talk about innovation these days, we know how things really are. It's way too easy for us to set up IT processes and procedures that we use to run our IT shops and then over time they become part of a larger "That's The Way We Do Things Here" culture.

The problem with this is that over time things change. Solutions that were once the best way to do things may no longer be the correct way to be doing something. However, we get caught in our ways and that starts to slow the whole IT department down and then the whole company.

Toyota has found a way around this problem that we can all learn from. They've come up with innovative ways to keep their IT employees constantly thinking about how the company can reach out and get new customers, enter new market segments, enter new geographic regions. Additionally, employees are challenged to consider better ways for the company to go after competitors, as well as how to create new ideas and come up with new and better practices.

How does Toyota accomplish all of this? One way is that they set nearly unattainable goals for the company. These goals are what push the company to overcome its existing routines and achieve new levels of performance. One such goal is stated as delivering "a full line in every market". This is nearly impossible for Toyota (or any car company) to do, but it does a great job of making all employees feel as though they are working together to achieve a common goal.

Toyota's goals are vague – on purpose. Goals like "create a cleaner car" don't have clear, nailed-down requirements. By doing this Toyota ensures that employees won't be able to look at a goal and say to themselves "that goal doesn't apply to me". Instead, vague goals result in multiple departments ending up working together in order try to achieve the goals.

What's interesting about Toyota's cars which are sold globally is that they aren't modified to meet local needs. Instead, Toyota takes the time to customize its products to meet the level of consumer sophistication that is found in each country.

IT needs to adopt this way of thinking: how can we modify the way a user interacts with an application to reflect what department they are in? Finance may need sophisticated reporting tools, but sales probably does not.

One of Toyota's greatest strengths is that it has built a culture in which there is an eagerness to take risks. This excitement about trying new ways to accomplish tasks is what allows Toyota to overcome those things that are blocking it from achieving its almost impossible goals.

Unlike so many other companies, Toyota is not constantly "betting the farm" on massive new projects. Instead, they have adopted a process by which they come up with big plans that they then go about implementing by taking a series of small steps.

This approach coupled with a philosophy of never giving up has allowed Toyota to be successful. When Toyota was developing an environmentally friendly car, they had a lot of failures – engines wouldn't start, batteries died, etc. However, they never gave up and the Prius was eventually created. Even this car is not the final result, but is rather a stepping stone towards where Toyota wants to get to.

Toyota's embrace of experimentation has not been done willy-nilly. Rather, they have a structured process called Plan-Do-Check-Act (PDCA) that is baked into their business processes.

What makes Toyota different is that employees are encouraged to speak up when something fails or when they run into a unsolvable problem. Toyota's culture of open communication has a great deal to teach all IT departments.

Chapter 8

What Toyota Can Teach IT About Dealing With Change

Chapter 8: What Toyota Can Teach IT About Dealing With Change

It may seem odd to be talking about growth during this time of economic downturn, but once this cycle is done you had better have a good plan for learning to deal with growth. IT has always been about change, but that doesn't mean that IT leaders are any better than anyone else in dealing with constant change (and growth).

We've been talking about Toyota lately and interestingly enough they have a great deal that they can teach IT about how to deal with change and growth. They realize that as an organization becomes larger, communication is one of the first things that will start to deteriorate. After this, it starts to become more difficult to coordinate operations and projects that stretch across the entire company.

In order to deal with problems such as these, Toyota has implemented three separate "forces of integration" that have allowed Toyota's IT department to be able to keep its focus on Toyota's mission. These three forces are the founder's original values, how they manage promotions, and their use of open communication. No high-tech stuff here, but perhaps they still have something to teach IT departments...

The values that have been handed down to Toyota by their founders include the famous kaizen (continuous improvement), respect for fellow employees and what they can accomplish, the power of teamwork, the spirit of humility, the importance of putting the customer first, and finally, just how important it is to see something with your own eyes.

Developing the next round of IT department leaders is done differently at every company. All too often, firms use the "up-or-out" approach – either you get promoted or you eventually get shown the door. This is not the way that Toyota runs their business.

Toyota actually still has a basic guarantee of lifetime employment for its workers. Employees who are under performing are not terminated, rather they have their capabilities upgraded through on the job training. At Toyota, IT workers are asked to think as if they were really operating at two levels above their current rank. This allows all employees to have more context added to their perspective.

Open communication is critical to everything that Toyota does. They have actually been able to accomplish what every IT department would like to do: have information flow freely both up and down the hierarchy as well as across both seniority and functional boundaries.

In the 21st Century, Toyota still feels that human to human networks are of the highest importance. Executives go to the lowest levels in the company and have discussions with the workers there in order to understand what is going on.

At Toyota it's ok for IT workers to speak up when they disagree with what someone is saying – even if it's their boss. The ultimate assignment for every employee is to do what they think is right – not just what the boss is telling them to do.

In the end, Toyota is a hard company for any IT department to try to emulate. The reason for this is because Toyota's success does not just come from doing (or not doing) any one thing. Instead, it's really about a culture that Toyota has created that allows all of its departments to be a success. Even though it may seem impossible to replicate this environment in your IT department, keep in mind that at Toyota they view trying as the greatest achievement and failure is just one step towards success.

Chapter 9

Citi Shows How NOT To Run An IT Department

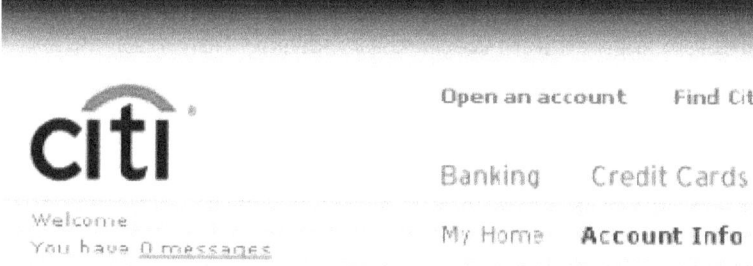

Chapter 9: Citi Shows How NOT To Run An IT Department

The news is always filled with IT departments that are winning awards for being innovative, reducing costs, or saving the day. That's why a recent article in the Wall Street Journal about how the Citi group's IT department is blowing it was so interesting...

The article was titled "Computer Glitch Slows Citi" (if you worked in Citi's IT department, you'd know that this couldn't be a good thing). It turns out that the retail bank part of the huge Citigroup Corporation had computer problems on this past Tuesday. These computer problems ended up leaving lots of customers and employees in a bind – they couldn't access information about bank accounts and mortgages.

It's bad enough to have problems like this; however, this problem lingered until Wednesday morning. Now in all fairness to Citi, it appears as though customers were still able to deposit, withdraw, and transfer funds during this period.

So in many other businesses, this type of outage would be no big deal. However, when you are one of the largest consumer banks in the country, this is most defiantly a no-no.

Just to make a bad thing worse, in the article Citigroup employees stated that their company seems especially plagued by crashes.

So who's to blame for this IT mess? It turns out that Citigroup Chief Executive Vikram Pandit has stepped up. He has promised to upgrade and integrate the company's computer systems. This effort is going to take several years and will probably end up costing billions of dollars.

What's missing from all of this is any word from Kevin Kessinger who is Citi's Chief Operations & Technology Officer. This is a fancy title for someone who has CIO responsibilities. At the end of the day, this mess is Kevin's responsibility.

The ability to keep a firm's basic applications up and running is so fundamental that we often refer to it as "blocking and tackling". This is an American football term that simply means that you need to play good defense before you spend anytime focusing on offense.

There is NO WAY that the Citi IT department should be working on anything else if their apps are not staying up. I'm sure that many of us spend time throwing rocks at our own IT departments for not being innovative enough; however, hopefully most of us do a good job of taking care of the basics.

Kevin has been in his job since 2005 and so he really does not have any excuse for not having already taken care of this problem. It's easy to throw stones at Kevin for not doing his job. However, perhaps it would be more valuable to take a look at what he should be doing right now to fix this issue:

- **Make App Stability THE Top Priority**: By communicating to the entire IT department that keeping apps up and running is job #1, this would send a clear message to everyone that this is what they need to be working on.

- **Appoint A Stability Czar**: Kevin needs to pick out an up-and-coming IT manager and put him / her in charge of working across the IT department to make sure that all of the apps become stable. This could be a career maker / breaker for this individual.

- **Change How Apps Are Developed:** The current problems are caused by how the current set of apps were developed. Clearly, a new set of design procedure and / or testing needs to be put into place.

Kevin probably needs to do a lot more than just these basic steps, but this is how he needs to start. The CIO is responsible for how the digital side of the company operates. Let's see if Kevin ends up doing the right thing...

Chapter 10

How To Drive An IT Department Into The Ground

Chapter 10: How To Drive An IT Department Into The Ground

You can go just about anywhere on the web or in your local bookstore and find ways to make your IT department a success. However, clearly this is not an easy thing to do when you take a moment to consider how much time that we spend trying to be successful.

What's missing from all of this is that you need to understand how people have failed at this task in order to understand what you need to do in order to succeed. How about if we take a look at some of the classic ways that IT departments have failed big time?

- **Fake Synergies:** All companies love this one – let's merge with someone who has complementary strengths in order to grow. However, this rarely seems to work for IT departments. Sometimes synergies do actually exist; however, this can be even worse because it can cause an IT department to head off in the wrong direction. Getting access to new customers or delivery systems can seem like a good idea, until AFTER the merger.

- **Questionable Financial Engineering**: We've all see this one show up at the end of a quarter or a fiscal year. Getting aggressive in how accounting is done won't necessarily land someone (you) in jail, but it can cause you some sleepless nights. The two big problems that getting creative with your company / department's financing is that they can cause you to believe in a product that is less than perfect and they can cause you to take on more risk – a move that the current downturn shows can be very risky.

- **Sticking With A Strategy Too Long**: Tenacity has long been considered to be a key asset of IT leaders. However, if you are going in the wrong direction in the first place, then this can lead to disaster. There is a secret at work here: the reason that IT departments don't change course is because the economics of doing things the new way don't measure up to the economics of doing things the old way.

- **"It's Just A Step To The Left"**: Often companies and IT departments decide that they need to try to sell new products to their existing customers or maybe through new channels (sometimes called an "adjacent-market" strategy). However, sometimes this is a bad idea that can bring down a department. You can tell that this is a bad idea if you are considering making this move not because it's a good business opportunity, but rather because your core business is having problems.

- **Selecting The Wrong Technology**: This one we all should recognize – betting on BetaMax when VHS ends up winning.

- **Consolidating Too Quickly**: All too often companies rush to consolidate when markets are maturing and the number of companies in the market start to shrink. Keeping in mind that when you buy a company you not only get its IT department, but you also get all of the problems that come along with it.

An IT department is just a part of a larger organization. However, both the company and the IT department are responsible for the overall success of the company. If you can avoid making these mistakes then you will that much closer to being successful!

Chapter 11

3 Secrets That Oil Companies Use To Run A Great IT Department

Chapter 11: 3 Secrets That Oil Companies Use To Run A Great IT Department

If you had to guess as to what the secret of running a great IT department is, what would you say? Peter Whatnell over at Sunoco has some thoughts on this subject. Peter breaks it down to three key items: knowing how your company makes money, choosing to not run against the company's culture, and remembering to never fall in love with technology. How hard can that be?

Whatnell is a bright guy: he's been in charge of Sunoco's IT operations since 2001 (remember the dot.com crash?) and he is now the president of the Society for Information Management. Ben Worthen over at the Wall Street Journal recently had a chance to sit down with Peter and have a chat about the role that an IT department plays in a company's success.

Whatnell pointed out that the arrival of a global recession has caused all IT departments to take any plans that they had created prior to the end of August and basically throw them away. The big hit is going to be especially felt in new projects.

The difference between current events and the dot.com crash that happened back in 2001 is that that crash really only impacted the IT community. This time around, it's really a global meltdown and it's impacting the whole business.

IT is facing a significant challenge in that there is now a lot of easy-to-use IT technology that is available to consumers. Examples include the iPhone (of course!) and free on-line email accounts with virtually unlimited storage. What this means is that corporate users are now expecting to see similar products available to them while they are at work.

IT departments have some valid security and support issues for not diving headlong into offering such services internally. However, they do need to seriously consider how to offer their customers such services.

Whatnell stresses that we need to make sure that we don't "…waste a good crisis." What he means by this is that 2009 is going to be tough and it's going to force every IT department to investigate nontraditional ways of delivering IT services.

Whatnell is somewhat famous for saying that he'd consider moving to a cheaper alternative, such as Google's email system, if he could get 90% of the functionality for 10% of the cost. One of the reasons that he's taken this stance is because he realizes that most users only scratch the surface of the functionality of the applications that they have available to them. Give the power users access to the fancy, expensive version of the apps and give everyone else the basic version.

Whatnell has some very specific thoughts when it comes to evaluating potential IT projects. He says that he evaluates projects based on what they do to support the company's strategy, what the business case is, and finally, what the business risk is.

He points out that the more change that an IT project would cause to how business is conducted, the bigger the risk is. This does not mean that you don't do the IT project, but that you need to be very careful and make sure that you give your full attention to all of the change management activities that would be required.

Chapter 12

Can't We All Just Get Along (In IT)?

Chapter 12: Can't We All Just Get Along (In IT)?

So there you are, manning the laptop, doing your utmost best to guide your IT department and, of course, your company on to greater glories. Do you really need to network with your colleagues at other firms? For that matter, do they really have anything to teach you?

Peter Whatnell over at Sunoco has some thoughts on this subject. Whatnell is a bright guy: he's been in charge of Sunoco's IT operations since 2001 (remember the dot.com crash?) and he is now the president of the Society for Information Management. Ben Worthen over at the Wall Street Journal recently had a chance to sit down with Peter and have a chat about the importance of remembering to look outside the company for ideas.

Whatnell makes the good point that the colleagues that you network with don't even have to be in the same industry as yourself. As an example, if you talk with someone who is working in IT for the construction industry and they start to mention how they are starting to use mobile devices to quickly distribute design changes, then you may have found an idea that you can use in your neck of the woods.

One of the big questions that we all deal with is "am I giving away competitive information if I talk shop with a colleague from another firm?" Whatnell makes the point that by now we should all be able to realize that what makes our firms competitive is not the underlying technology that we use. Talking about technology is not going to reveal any big company secrets.

What makes our firms competitive is how we go about using these pieces of technology in order to solve the problems that our firm is facing. This means that even if you and your competitor have access to the same technology, you'll end up putting it together much differently.

Whatnell believes that the true source of a competitive advantage is knowing exactly how you can use IT to help make your business more successful. One interesting way to do this is to ask key executives how the firm makes money. If they don't know, then this is an area that IT can help simplify.

In these tough times, it's interesting to hear what Whatnell has to say about what his biggest challenge is. Sunoco is an oil company – it's a commodity business that's competing in a mature market. In order for Sunoco to be successful, the firm is going to have to find a way to become THE low cost provider.

What this means for IT is that we need to find ways to help the business side of the house cut expenses, reduce cycle times, and improve their overall agility. The goal should be to avoid having IT being told to just "cut your budget to help our bottom line."

In the end, Whatnell says that an IT department needs to have earned its credibility within the company in order to be able to be able to contribute to helping the company reduce costs. The key here is that you need to have already earned this credibility.

It's from the forge of failure that the steel of success is formed.

Hard Work Does Not Guarantee Success, But Success Does Not Happen Without Hard Work.

- Dr. Jim Anderson

Create IT Departments That Are Productive And A Valuable Asset To The Rest Of The Company !

Dr. Jim Anderson is available to provide training and coaching on the topics that are the most important to people who have to manage IT departments: how can I build a productive IT department (and keep it together) while at the same time providing the rest of the company with the IT services that they need?

Dr. Anderson believes that in order to both learn and remember what he says, speakers need to laugh. Each one of his speeches is full of fun and humor so that what he says "sticks" with everyone.

Dr. Anderson's CIO SkillsTraining Includes:

4. How to identify and attract the right type of IT workers to your IT department.
5. How to build relationships with the company's senior management in order to get the support that you need?
6. How to stay on top of changing technology and security issues so that you never get surprised?

Dr. Jim Anderson works with over 100 customers per year. To invite Dr. Anderson to work with you, contact him at:

Phone: 813-418-6970 or
Email: jim@BlueElephantConsulting.com

Photo Credits:

Cover - Quinn Dombrowski
https://www.flickr.com/photos/quinnanya/

Chapter 1 - The U.S. Army
https://www.flickr.com/photos/soldiersmediacenter/

Chapter 2 - Stuart Caie
https://www.flickr.com/photos/kyz/

Chapter 3 - UWI Seismic Research Centre
https://www.flickr.com/photos/seismicresearchcentre/

Chapter 4 - 401(K) 2012
https://www.flickr.com/photos/68751915@N05/

Chapter 5 - Mike Mozart
https://www.flickr.com/photos/jeepersmedia/

Chapter 6 – Daniel
https://www.flickr.com/photos/danielctw/

Chapter 7 - keso s
https://www.flickr.com/photos/keso/

Chapter 8 - lpk 90901
https://www.flickr.com/photos/lpk90901/

Chapter 9 - lobstar28
https://www.flickr.com/photos/lobstar/

Chapter 10 - burlington_rc
https://www.flickr.com/photos/brcf/

Chapter 11 – bsheets
https://www.flickr.com/photos/bsheets/

Chapter 12 - Florent Darrault
https://www.flickr.com/photos/workflo/

Other Books By The Author

Product Management

- Product Development Lessons For Product Managers: How Product Managers Can Create Successful Products

- Customer Lessons For Product Managers: Techniques For Product Managers To Better Understand What Their Customers Really Want

- Product Failure Lessons For Product Managers: Examples Of Products That Have Failed For Product Managers To Learn From

- Communication Skills For Product Managers: The Communication Skills That Product Managers Need To Know How To Use In Order To Have A Successful Product

- How To Have A Successful Product Manager Career: The Things That You Need To Be Doing TODAY In Order To Have A Successful Product Manager Career

- Product Manager Product Success: How to keep your product on track and make it become a success

Public Speaking

- How To Give A Great Presentation: Presentation techniques that will transform a speech into a memorable event

- How To Rehearse In Order To Give The Perfect Speech: How to effectively rehearse your next speech to that your message be remembered forever!

- Secrets To Creating The Perfect Speech: How to create a speech that will make your message be remembered forever!

- Secrets To Organizing The Perfect Speech: How to organize the best speech of your life!

- Secrets To Planning The Perfect Speech: How to plan to give the best speech of your life

- Delivering Excellence: How To Give Presentations That Make A Difference

CIO Skills

- How CIOs Can Make Innovation Happen: Tips And Techniques For CIOs To Use In Order To Make Innovation Happen In Their IT Department

- CIO Communication Skills Secrets: Tips And Techniques For CIOs To Use In Order To Become Better Communicators

- Managing Your CIO Career: Steps That CIOs Have To Take In Order To Have A Long And Successful Career

- CIO Business Skills: How CIOs can work effectively with the rest of the company!

IT Manager Skills

- Secrets Of Effective Leadership For IT Managers: Tips And Techniques That IT Managers Can Use In Order To Develop Leadership Skills

- IT Manager Career Secrets: Tips And Techniques That IT Managers Can Use In Order To Have A Successful Career

- IT Manager Budgeting Skills: How IT Managers Can Request, Manage, Use, And Track Their Funding

Negotiating

- Learn How To Argue In Your Next Negotiation: How To Develop The Skill Of Effective Arguing In A Negotiation In Order To Get The Best Possible Outcome

- How To Open Your Next Negotiation: How To Start A Negotiation In Order To Get The Best Possible Outcome

- Preparing For Your Next Negotiation: What You Need To Do BEFORE A Negotiation Starts In Order To Get The Best Possible Deal

Miscellaneous

- Power Distribution Unit (PDU) Secrets: What Everyone Who Works In A Data Center Needs To Know!

- Making The Jump: How To Land Your Dream Job When You Get Out Of College!

Decision Making Skills That Every CIO Needs To Have In Order To Be Able To Make The Right Choices

This book has been written with one goal in mind – to show you how you successfully manage your IT department. It's not easy being a CIO so we're going to show you the strategies and techniques that you can use to make sure that you make the right decisions for your IT department!

Let's Make Your CIO Career A Success!

What You'll Find Inside:

- **CIO LESSONS FROM THE WAR IN IRAQ**

- **RISK MANAGEMENT IN IT: HOW DO YOU DO IT CORRECTLY?**

- **WHY TOYOTA'S IT DEPARTMENT IS BROKEN & WHY THAT'S OK**

- **3 SECRETS THAT OIL COMPANIES USE TO RUN A GREAT IT DEPARTMENT**

Dr. Jim Anderson brings his 25 years of real-world experience to this book. He's been a senior IT executive at some of the world's largest firms. He's going to show you what you need to do (and not do!) in order to make your CIO career a success!

www.ingramcontent.com/pod-product-compliance
Lightning Source LLC
Chambersburg PA
CBHW061217180526
45170CB00003B/1046